Pickles, Poems, and Prayers

Hannah,

I have been blessed to have you in my life as we both grow together in christ. I love that you call me uncle Shawn, You are an amazing young lady, and ~~you~~ will always have a special place in my heart. Really enjoy our dinner dates / one on one time.

Be a reflection
Not a deflection,

"Uncle" Shawn Coo

Pickles, Poems, and Prayers

Shawn Cook

Copyright © 2015 Shawn Cook.

All rights reserved. No part of this book may be used or reproduced by any means, graphic, electronic, or mechanical, including photocopying, recording, taping or by any information storage retrieval system without the written permission of the publisher except in the case of brief quotations embodied in critical articles and reviews.

Archway Publishing books may be ordered through booksellers or by contacting:

Archway Publishing
1663 Liberty Drive
Bloomington, IN 47403
www.archwaypublishing.com
1 (888) 242-5904

Because of the dynamic nature of the Internet, any web addresses or links contained in this book may have changed since publication and may no longer be valid. The views expressed in this work are solely those of the author and do not necessarily reflect the views of the publisher, and the publisher hereby disclaims any responsibility for them.

Any people depicted in stock imagery provided by Thinkstock are models, and such images are being used for illustrative purposes only. Certain stock imagery © Thinkstock.

ISBN: 978-1-4808-1879-8 (sc)
ISBN: 978-1-4808-1880-4 (e)

Library of Congress Control Number: 2015908240

Print information available on the last page.

Archway Publishing rev. date: 05/20/2015

Contents

BC: Before I Found Christ written between 1987-1991.... 1

Trials and Tribulations written between 2010-2014 27

Desires of the Heart written between 2010-2014........ 87

AC: After I found Christ written between 2010-2014... 151

Bits and Pieces written between 2010-2014........... 205

My only hope through doing this is that one person finds Christ among all of this. I hope that one person realizes that no matter what they have done in life, God still loves them and is there for them. I know I had a hard time believing that, so I guess these poems are to help you realize that life is never hopeless unless you want it to be. I reached my breaking point before I found hope; I want you to find it sooner. Thanks to those that encouraged me to move forward with this; Karen, Dina, and Jane. Also want to thank those that helped guide my path back to Christ: Dave, Christine, Nathon, and Tonya. I write in honor of my daughters Christina, Lisa, and Tiffany, and my unborn child that I look forward to meeting in Heaven.

BC: Before I Found Christ

I'm not sure what started it all, but I got angry with God and lost all hope. Maybe it was my relationship with my father at the time, maybe my lack of self-confidence, or maybe just fate. Regardless of the cause and the effect at the time, and regardless of the thoughts in my head that there was no hope in Jesus Christ or God, I know now that He was there watching over me and guiding my path to keep me safe, waiting patiently for me to find Him. Broken, damaged, defeated, and wishing for nothing more than an end to the life I knew, I found Christ waiting to embrace me, to love me, and to help me realize that I was never really alone. I am neither proud nor ashamed of the writings in this first chapter; they are a part of my journey in life and helped to make me who I am today. Although incomplete, and having been written long before my next writing, this is all that remains of many years of life misspent. My only hope for these writings is that in the end, they all bring great joy to the world and open doors for others to find what I searched for my whole life.

Untitled #1

Twisted torment

In my brain!

Nothing seems

To kill the pain!

Take a knife

And run it through!

Is there nothing

Left to do?

Why such a

Twisted death?

Pain and suffering

With each breath!

My only thought:

To be free.

Is there nothing

Left of me?

I want to live,

And I want to die!

As my blood fills

The evening sky.

Is there nothing

Left of me?

Why couldn't they

Just let me be?

Memories Unspoken

My heart is broken

By thoughts, words, and deeds.

Memories unspoken

Are all I have left of me.

My body and soul

Are the wind and the breeze;

They float through the air

And whistle through the trees.

Loss of freedom

Would be like death to me

That's why it is

Alone I must be.

Until I find a woman

Who can understand me,

Who will give me the time

And space to be free.

Untitled #2

Loss of pain,

No feeling within.

Don't know where I'm going,

Can't say where I've been.

Lost in a dream,

A thought from within

Can't tell where it ends,

Don't know where to begin.

I would die to live,

But yet I live to die.

Nothing has been gained

Except loss of mind.

I have self-respect

But no respect for mankind.

I have no friends,

Yet I am never alone.

I tend to drink a lot,

And yes, I've been stoned.

I've answered all the questions

I thought you might ask

So all of you

Can kiss my ass!

Never asked to live,

Never wanted to die.

I hope you're not offended

By my freedom cry.

No one ever asked me

If I wanted to live and then die.

Untitled #3

Many thoughts run through my head,

But few of them are ever said.

No one knows how I feel

I hide behind a wall unreal.

No one wants to tear it down

They are afraid of what might be found.

Maybe a kind and decent man,

Or is he angry with evil plans?

Heaven sent, yet I await

A trip though hell's lonely gates—

Face to face with Satan I stand

Lucifer and Belial walk hand in hand

Leviathan looks on with evil plans,

Sweat pouring from every gland.

They all laugh and say I am wise,

That life is filled with only lies,

Few live and everyone dies,

That within me they have pride

For I am the one who never cried,

Never laughed or said good-bye.

They ask me to join their side,

To make their four an evil five.

I start to laugh; I've got my pride.

What makes you think I need you guys?

I'm the most evil, dead or alive,

I walk alone, never breaking stride.

Now I have my throne,

The lone ruler of the world unknown.

I am not a god or a devil,

Only the ruler of the world on the level.

Some say it's heaven, others say it's hell

Your mental status can break its spell

You can come and go as you please

There are no rules in the world I lead

No law to tell you right or wrong

Do as you wish before it's all gone.

Life and death do not occur

They are only a thought and then a blur.

Only my thoughts tell good from evil:

Without my thoughts, there are no people.

Untitled #4

Woke up this morning
With thoughts that brought on the day
Didn't think I could love anyone
Until I met you yesterday
Now every thought, sight, and dream
Of every night and every day
Is filled with visions of you
That just won't fade away
Every hope and every wish
Is that you will love me too someday
No matter how hard things get
You know my love will never stray
You know I will wait a lifetime
For those three words I wish you to say
I love you, I want you, and I need you
And if not, then alone I will stay.

In the morning, anyone
May dream of you.
I wish I could get
A lifetime with you.

Untitled #5

Misunderstood,

In each and every way

I still don't know

What I am doing today.

Lost in myself

Can't find a way out

Nobody hears

When I scream or shout!

No one cares

They say I've dug my grave.

If no love is expressed,

Then none will be craved.

I'm never alone,

Not even in bed

Thanks to all the voices

Running through my head.

Some say I should live

Others say die

Some tell me to laugh

Then I start to cry.

I was born into this world

As an angel in Mom's eye

She didn't realize until it was too late

That I was the devil in disguise.

I was born a total loser

But Mom thought I would arise

Didn't mean to disappoint her

Didn't mean to make her cry.

But when I turned sixteen,

Things started to decay

Drugs and alcohol warped my brain

As the devil in me got stronger day by day.

Mom told me I was changing—

I had turned to shades of gray

Didn't want to play anymore

And I didn't want to pray.

Don't want to live anymore

Don't even know my name

I think I'm going insane

They already dug my grave

Untitled #6

Tossed and turned all night
As demons ran through my head
Woke up in the morning
And the devil lay in my bed.
He told me he could give me anything,
But these words must be said:
"I will my soul to the devil
And I wish that I were dead."
I always trusted everybody
Never lied to anyone
But something in my heart told me
The devil wasn't out for fun.
I smiled at him for a little while
And then I began to run.
He yelled out, "You're a fool, boy,
'Cause now life has begun!"
I am under the gun
It gets harder day by day
But to help carry me through
To the Lord God I pray.

Sometimes when I lie in bed at night,

I think the devil is here to stay

But when I look out the window in the morning

I know that Jesus is the way.

Untitled #7

Psychedelic mind warp

Mental death

You cannot laugh

Without breath

LSD

Is what we crave

All the time

It's all the rave.

They sing and dance

And laugh a lot,

Take more acid,

Smoke some pot.

They watch

The laser lights till dawn.

No one knows

What's going on.

Why don't you

Suck down a nitrous balloon?

Psychedelic happiness

Is mental doom.

Untitled #8

Someday there will be

A world without people,

Without churches,

Without steeples.

No sun or moon

To bring us light,

Only the loneliness

Of the darkened night.

No God to tell us

Right from wrong,

No words to say,

No friendly song.

How does it feel

Being all alone?

Your only friend

Is a distant moan.

No smiles to see,

No hands to shake

No friends to enjoy

Or to forsake.

What is this place

Where we work and play?

Could it be

Hell isn't that far away?

Untitled #9

Imagine standing

In a gentle rain

'Neath the smiling face

From whence it came.

Imagine, if you would,

The pouring rain

As an angry face

Filled with pain.

I prefer

The smiling rain

That patters so softly

And massages my brain.

Oh, how I hate

The angry rain

That floods our world

And brings no gain.

Oh Lord, please,

Bring us gentle rain

Because life already has

Too much pain.

Untitled #10

Why does it come

As no surprise

That life is filled

With only lies?

No truth to any

Words we say

Only a false sense

That things are okay.

Everyone telling you

What's right and wrong.

Everything that seems right

Is always wrong.

I'm so confused

About life today;

If I thought it would help,

I'd probably pray.

But I see no way

Of saving face;

Made in God's image,

We are a disgrace.

If He could see us

And I know that He can

He would shed big tears

All over the land.

Untitled #11

Never-ending challenges

Always pushing to do more

Life is filled with questions

Different answers at every door

Everything so nerve-wracking

No peace in sight.

I wish I were a bird

Aloft in endless flight

Gliding through the air

Not caring what is right

Searching for some food

To slake my appetite

No cares or worries

Except for my survival

The only fear I have

Is of my deadly rivals.

The Religion of Love

Gods, Devils,

And Lords of the land

Are worshiped by all

In their own little clans.

But I follow no guidelines

Of belief

My religion is love

And it has no chief.

Only the heart

And soul will command

A piece of the mind

Can lend a helping hand.

There is no bible

With stories to tell

And sitting side by side

Are heaven and hell.

You will go through both

Before life is complete

And before you find true love

You will have admitted defeat.

Selfish

Searching for answers
Only to find more questions—
Unforeseen challenges—
Never to be complete.
Searching for the light
Only to find the darkness;
Trying to light the candle,
The wick is already burnt.
Searching for a friend
Only to find an enemy
Pondering love…
Happiness shouldn't hurt.
Searching for a family
Only to find loneliness
Walking in solitude
No destination to be found.
Searching for a kind soul
Only to find an empty heart
Never thought that pride
Would tear a world apart.

Untitled #12

Late at night

All alone

No one to see

No telephone

Just sitting here.

No music plays

No TV box

No one has

Anything to say.

I can feel my bones

Slowly decay

As skin and muscles

Just rot away.

Wrinkles forming

Upon my brow

Shriveled fingers

Can't move them now.

Untitled #13

If the sun doesn't rise tomorrow,
There will never be another day
But it doesn't matter to me.
Things just haven't gone my way.
Ever since I was a young boy
I've felt I was all alone
Misunderstood since the beginning
I guess you'd say I'm on my own.
Always tried to do things differently
Didn't like to follow stride
Had to do it my own way.
I was always filled with pride.
I will not follow in your footsteps
But I will walk by your side.
I didn't abide by all your rules
But I cried when you died.
I may not be the richest man
But by God I am alive
And I will take every kick I get
And by God I will survive.

Trials and Tribulations

Regardless of what we believe, we all go through trials and tribulations. Sometimes we get ourselves into a pickle at times where there seems to be no good way out. I can tell you from personal experience, the pickles become fewer the close I get to Christ. Hope becomes greater, faith becomes stronger, and love becomes more natural. Christians are not perfect, we still struggle every day and sometimes we still fail. At least we have Jesus in the end to guide us through.

Untitled #14

A dead man's moan

Has brought me here.

Don't make a sound,

Don't shed a tear

You have to face

Your mortal fear

For the evil one

Will soon be near.

Stand your ground

Don't walk away

For if you do

There'll be hell to pay.

I have no fear

As I walk though the flames

My past behind me

In smoke and acid rains.

Wash me clean

Again today

For it is to you, Lord,

I often pray.

I am blind

I cannot see

What it is, Lord,

You have planned for me;

It is only through

Faith I stand

For I am merely

A mortal man.

Untitled #15

Numb from life,

Numb from death!

Numb from every

Waking breath!

Feeling nothing

Anymore.

Turn the key,

Lock the door.

Come on, let your

Spirit sway

Just like the trees

On a windy day.

No feelings of lust

Or sexual gain,

No feelings of hate,

No feelings of pain.

Only feelings of love

For one and all.

Come fly with me

Let's have a ball.

Untitled #16

Oh, sweet, soft,

And gentle rain

Wash me clean

Cleanse my pain.

Take away the haunting

Of my brain.

Open my heart

To love unstained.

Wash away the demons

That try to burn my soul.

Fill me with your spirit,

And again make me whole.

I praise you, Lord,

With all that I do.

My focus in this life

Is for a life with you.

So let your rain come down

And touch my brow.

All that matters,

Is your with me now.

Untitled #17

He walks through life in silence,

Never whispering a word;

When he talked of the love of God,

His voice was never heard.

People labeled him a sinner

And rebuked the words he'd say

So he sits in a dark and lonely room

And for their souls he prays.

Prayer may not always be the answer,

But what an amazing place to start.

His thoughts are of the love of God

And the Holy Spirit fills his heart;

He walks through life with Jesus

And with God's grace today.

Still, the evil that surrounds him

Won't soon go away.

He may often stumble,

And occasionally he may fall

But it is through his love for Christ

That he will rise above it all.

Untitled #18

I was blinded by your light today.

I didn't even see you come

With a head full of heartaches

And a belly full of rum.

I am surely not the prince of peace

I'm a pauper yet today.

I've never followed the beaten path

Just done it my own way;

I've shouldered all my heartaches

Carried my burdens every day.

But when I gave them all to you,

You took them all away.

I would have never thought

I'd feel the way I do—

But almighty God,

I owe it all to you.

Untitled #19

I have no faith

I have no hope

On winds of time

I begin to choke

I did not turn

I did not run

As I found

Eternal numb.

Broken and battered

Is this my fate?

Do I embrace the love

Or succumb to hate?

Ever since

I left the womb

Satan's tests

Eternal doom.

With one desperate cry

I reached out my hand

Won't you save me,

Son of Man?

Then I died

And was born again

Back into God's

Eternal plan.

Without faith

There is no hope

That's why Jesus

Is my rope.

Untitled #20

If you looked out my window
And saw my life before
You would look at me in horror
And never unlock the door.
I filled my walls with anguish
I filled my walls with pain
I filled my walls with evil
And lustful, selfish gain.
But I believe in evolution
And that God can unlock all doors;
He lifted up this broken spirit
From the man I was before.
Now I lay my faith in Jesus.
Upon the cross I hang my shame.
I will always be a sinner
And Christian is my name.

Untitled #21

Would God create a man

To live and die alone?

He is just a mortal creature

Of flesh, skin, and bone.

He walks through life in silence;

With people lie his fears

Because of all the pain he felt

For so very many years.

They called him a weirdo

A loser and a freak

But he is more of a lover—

Like a bird that can not speak.

He does not carry a weapon;

Silence is his shield

And certain parts of his life

May never be revealed.

As he looks up to the heavens,

He raises his arms in joy

For only the power of Jesus

Can make a man a boy.

Through the Holy Spirit

Silence has no shame

With a gentle touch and smile

Love the man became.

Untitled #22

I sit here alone, Lord,

Again today

Waiting for you, Lord,

To take me away.

I'm tired of this world—

That's plain to see;

Up there with you, Lord,

Is where I want to be.

Just sitting here, Lord,

Wasting away

I raise my hands to the heavens,

And to you, Lord, I pray:

Come and get me, Lord,

Take me away;

At home in your spirit

I spend today;

Within your presence

I want to stay.

Away from you, Lord,

I will never stray.

I raise my hands to the heavens,
    And to you, Lord, I pray:
    Come and get me, Lord,
        Just take me away.

Untitled #23

Have you ever tasted loneliness

No matter who or what was around?

Have you ever smelled brimstone and burnt flesh

Or been chased by Satan's hounds?

Within my mind, I've been so many places

That you may never see;

I've touched the hand of Satan

And know who he wants to be.

I've felt the pain of death,

I've lived the bondage of sin;

I know where one world ends

And where the next begins.

Satan pulls on one hand,

Jesus touches the other with care:

They both want your heart and soul,

Even when nobody else is there.

Untitled #24

To give and to give—

Yes, of your life, in a cell.

You cannot drink

From an empty well.

Are you going to heaven

Or will it be hell?

It will be easy to figure

If you can't stand the smell.

What is bought and sold

But is never for sale?

I try and I try,

But so often I fail.

It is hard to balance

On only one rail.

I stand all alone

With no story or tale.

I look for the right

But always find the wrong.

Do I sit here in tears

Or sing a sweet song?

I wake up and I breathe

And I continue along

To be by your side—

Have I waited too long?

Untitled #25

Satan laughing

Broken stare

It is he who knows not

When or where.

They start to yell

They begin to fight

They do this dance

Throughout the night.

Lovers quarrel

Poets dream

It must be true—

Or so it seems.

Broken glass

Turn out the light

It is we who choose

To love or fight.

No words are spoken

A quiet glare

With open arms

We make a pair.

Satan crying

Hollow stare

It's Jesus' love

That we must share.

Untitled #26

I feel you crying

Within my heart.

I feel your pain

From worlds apart.

Broken and beaten,

Inside and out

I don't know whether

To scream or shout.

All this pain

I cannot bear.

From whence it comes

I know not where.

Darkness fills

An empty room.

Broken spirit

Cascades of gloom.

When all hope is gone

And out of sight

Raise your hands,

Toward the light.

Untitled #27

Pain and darkness,

Go away

Don't come back

Again to stay.

I will mix a potion

Of love and hope

Throw in some faith

To make it smoke

And watch as my demons

Begin to choke.

They can't handle the power

Of love and hope

And from my faith,

they run in fear

Because of the God

I hold so dear.

Untitled #28

Demon blood

Runs through his veins

Pumping lust

And selfish gains

Not separating

Wrong from right

Just seeking

To quench his appetite

Filling up

On lust and greed

Nothing seems

To kill his need

Earthly treasures

And plunders abound

Another square peg

In a world of round.

Then he hears

What Jesus said

The cleansing blood

The breaking bread

The Holy Spirit

Fills his heart

Filtering out

These shades of dark

Always knowing

Right from wrong

Filled with love

He trudges along

When his thoughts

Become absurd

The spirit gives

A guiding word.

A deep breath

Brings on the day

If you listen closely

You can hear him pray.

Worldly Sorrow

Sorrow lives

But never dies.

Too many hellos

And no goodbyes.

Broken-hearted

Empty dreams;

Outside smiles,

Inside screams.

Battered spirit,

Tortured soul.

Worldly life,

Graveyard hole.

Sorrow fills

The empty heart.

Blood-stained, spattered,

Shades of dark.

It's hard to see

The light of day;

What comes and goes

Won't stay away.

Weak and wounded
By chains be bound
The licking lips
Of Satan's hounds.
Worldly happiness
Will never be found.
Jesus is the key
To chains unbound.

Untitled #29

Lord,

I carry my pains—so many—

And I live with my burdens too.

Sometimes I just wish for

Another few moments with you.

You give me something to hope for,

And dreams that may never come true

But yet I still lay my faith in

A much better plan from you.

I search for the love of a lifetime;

If it is in your plans, it will be.

Even though I search for a flower,

A branch of your vine I will be.

If I just asked for her heart,

It would be just her and me;

But I also ask for your heart

To make it a trinity.

Untitled #30

Comfort of a father's hand.

Will I ever love again?

Broken will and wounded heart

I just don't know where to start

Not once or twice but thrice I found

My heart and soul beat to the ground.

But yet inside I hold out hope

For a love so strong it needs no rope.

When I think of you I start to shake;

The butterflies inside do awake.

Will I even be able to say hi

If you ever pass me by?

Will I ever catch your eye?

Or will a babbling fool stay I?

I really hope I don't mess this up:

A hound by sight, by heart a pup.

Down Day

If I could just

Have my way

I would give

My life away.

Not really sure

Why I'm so down

Could be that my love

Just left town.

Or is it just because

I am back in this place again

Where no one I can see

Would consider me a friend.

Lord, please come

And take me away;

If you do

I'd send a smile your way.

Or is it just that

It's Monday again?

I hope that soon

This day will end.

Untitled #31

Was I destined

To be alone?

Like the moss

That grows flat

On a rolling stone.

Or was I destined

To be more?

Like a great hero

Who died

In the war.

I am just

An average man

Today.

Watching as life

Slowly slips

Away.

Is my life ending,

Or has it

Just begun?

Because now the devil

    Is the one

    On the run.

Untitled #32

I came from

My mother's womb

A gentle man

In an emotional tomb.

Don't show you care

Or you will pay the price

Because the pain you feel

Is but a small sacrifice.

Why do some people

Want to smile and say

It makes them feel good

To take my dreams away.

Why should I

Even dream anymore?

Behind every dream

Is another locked door.

Someone else

Always holds the key

Why can't they

Just let me be?

Please just let me

Follow one dream through.

The dream I would pick

Is to spend time with you.

Untitled #33

Run from

What is real.

Don't let anyone

Know how you feel.

Give a little

Or give a lot;

When judgment comes,

You will soon be forgot.

Wear a smile

On the outside

Keep the twisted torment

Locked up inside.

Always wear

Your poker face

Cause if you show the truth

You will be a disgrace.

Could someone please

Take my breath away?

I don't feel the need to breathe

Yet another day.

Just let me drift off

And fade away.

Life will be the same tomorrow

As it is today.

Untitled #34

Don't look into my eyes too deeply

Unless you want to know what they have to say.

I've been hurt many times, so completely

That the pain just won't melt away.

I am a quiet man filled with passion;

A fire burns in me everyday.

You cannot find true love

Unless you're willing to give your heart away.

I am nothing special

Just an average man

Walking though life in silence

With strong, yet gentle, hands.

So if you ever look my way

And decide to give me a chance

I promise you wont forget

The way I made your heart dance.

Untitled #35

Every time a tear drops

Every time it rains

Thoughts of mental anguish

Get locked inside my brain.

I don't come to you with answers

But I feel your mortal pain;

Sometimes we think we've lost it all

And there is nothing left to gain.

We try to hide our feelings—

Wouldn't want the world to know

That locked away deep down inside

Is an emotional rodeo.

As you sit there in the darkness

You should know you're not alone;

Why don't you just give me a call?

I'll be waiting by the phone.

Untitled #36

True friends in life

Are hard to find;

I'm proud to say

You're one of mine.

You're a special person

Both bold and true.

We need more people in this world

Who are just like you.

You're fun and sweet,

You're caring and kind;

A very rare combination

To find.

I guess the thing

I'm trying to say

Is have a Merry Christmas

And a happy holiday.

Untitled #37

Do not wake

The sleeping dog

For he might

Bite you through the fog.

A purple haze

May appear

Between you and the one

You hold most dear.

The thoughts

Inside my brain

Are not what's

Driving me insane.

But here is

Another thought:

What can be sold,

But can't be bought?

It is your soul

They want to take

From the one

You can't forsake.

Untitled #38

When your life

Is in a bog

Listen to

The cricket and the frog.

They will tell you

About their day

And how their

Whole world is okay;

About the water

In the pond

And how they'd prefer

You not mow the lawn;

About the wonderful

Spring breeze

And how the sun

Didn't let them freeze;

About the snake

In the grass

And how the whole world

Can kiss their ass;

About the troubles

That they face

Not being part

Of the human race.

Untitled #39

Sometimes I sit

And wonder why

Life just seems

To pass me by.

It used to be

I'd take a toke,

Have a drink,

Or snort some coke;

Take some acid

And melt my brain—

I'd get so high,

I'd feel no pain.

It used to be

I'd sit and say,

What became of

Yesterday?

In the devil's playground

I used to run;

No harm done,

We were just having fun.

Now sometimes

I will sit and pray

And I will shed a tear

For yesterday.

Is my life

Over and done?

Or has a new life

Just begun?

Untitled #40

Fear of life

Fear of death

Fear of every

Waking breath.

Grab a knife,

Run it through;

Kill the beast

Inside of you.

I cannot live

Another day

If in this world

I have to stay.

Can you ever really

Escape from reality?

Is anyone safe?

Is anyone free?

Twisted thoughts,

Rotting brains;

Is there nothing left

To kill the pain?

I close my eyes

I start to pray.

Why must life

Be this way?

Broken hearts

Empty dreams

A lifeless life—

Or so it seems.

Breathe in,

Breathe out

As the voices

Scream and shout.

Will it start

Or end today?

I'm done with life.

I don't want to play.

Untitled #41

You're a weirdo

You're a freak

You're a never-ending geek

You're a loser

You're a chump

Just sit back and take your lumps

You're all alone

You wonder why

As they all just pass you by

There's the moon

There's the sun

As they all start to run

You wave hello

You wave goodbye

And you never bat an eye

Nothing here

Nothing there

Why don't you just grow a pair?

Is it you?

Is it me?

Was it ever meant to be?

Untitled #42

Falling, falling,

Forever more!

Will I ever

Reach the floor?

Broken, beaten,

And battered today!

Will I always

Feel this way?

Falling, falling,

Never more.

Blood stains cover

An empty floor.

No way in

No way out

Is this what they mean

By "down and out"?

Laughing, crying,

Every day.

If this wasn't life,

It wouldn't be this way.

Falling, falling,

Forever more.

Goodbye now—

Shut the door.

Untitled #43

The weeds of wrath
Have spun their net
But for the life I lead,
I have no regret.
An empty thimble
To the naked eye,
Sorrow and death
Have passed him by.
Who is this man?
It is but I.
Somebody's nobody,
Without even a sigh.
He slayed his demons,
The devil be told,
For he worships a God
Much greater than gold.
In silence and torment,
He laid down his shame;
He knelt at the cross
And called out God's name.

Somebody's nobody
Is what they might see,
But he is a somebody
And within, he feels free.

Untitled #44

I live in the realm

Of a man unknown.

I enter a realm

Of mere flesh and bone:

A lust for life

And time misspent;

I'd sacrifice the day

For a night hell-bent.

It's hard to believe

I was heaven-sent,

Destroying hope

Just to pay the rent.

Angel eyes

And demon skies;

What comes and goes,

But never dies?

Lustful thoughts

And lustful deeds

A lustful world

Filled with needs:

A need for this,

A need for that—

We need it all!

Our egos are fat.

Never full,

Always wanting more:

Satan laughs

At what's in store.

Untitled #45

Locked inside

An open door

This fleshly world

Cries for more.

A carnal cell

Of mortal doom,

He is never full—

An empty tomb.

His need to feed

Is your pain;

The broken creed

Is driving him insane.

His hell

His cell

He refuses

The pain.

Broken spirit

Broken dream

Beyond repair—

Or so it seems.

The Word:

Now I see.

The Word:

I belong to thee.

Through hope

And faith

What a love

I have found.

Untitled #46

Locked inside

This fleshly cell

Broken arrow

Living hell.

Some they roam;

Me, I dwell

Shut up in

My fleshly hell.

Holy Spirit,

Guide my way

Away from what

This world may say.

No matter what

My sins today,

Jesus Christ

Will guide my way.

Untitled #47

Dragonfly,

Don't say goodbye.

There is no rhyme

Or reason why

You fly about

From leaf to leaf,

Not worrying what

Lies above or beneath.

You set a twinkle

In an old man's eye

Of a child's life:

A mental sigh.

The fondest memories

Of my best friends,

Days that start

And never end:

We'd play from dawn

Till well after dark,

No worries or cares

In God's ballpark,

Our biggest problem

A wounded knee—

Days of joy

And nights of glee.

Oh dragonfly,

Don't say goodbye.

I love where

You help me fly.

Untitled #48

A way with words—

Oh, words that weigh!

We play them each

And every day:

Some softly spoken,

Others harshly slung;

What has been dealt

Can't be undone.

Some laced with love,

Others said with hate:

Before you speak,

Take time to wait

Five deep breaths

And four ho hums—

Clear your broken mind

Before a sentence is begun.

Swords of the tongue

Strike a mighty blow;

No drop of blood,

But damage to the soul.

Untitled #49

Lost in love

Lost in grace

Lost in this world

Lost in this place

Lost in you

Lost in me—

Unending love

Set me free.

Lost in desire

Human is my heart

Why do I let it

Tear me apart?

Why can I not

Just focus on you?

Why can't I be satisfied

With a love that is true?

Untitled #50

Men on white horses

Came to take me away.

Not sure where I'm going

Don't know what to say.

I still wonder what it was

Or if I'll see you once more;

My heart, it remembers

As my face hits the floor.

I don't have a big mansion,

But my thoughts are not poor;

I know you are leaving,

But don't shut the door.

I catch myself dreaming

About you again today;

Like childhood memories,

In my heart you will stay.

I'm not sure what it is

That draws me to you

But the door is still open

And I'm yearning for you.

Desires of the Heart

Sometimes we get lost in our own desires and do not take into consideration God's desires for us. I have been lost many a time in the eyes of a woman before and after I found Christ in my life. A broken heart is a terrible thing, but fearful heart is lost forever.

Untitled #51

I would walk

A thousand miles

Just to see

Your beautiful smile;

You have meant so much to me

Throughout the years.

Through your eyes,

I shed no tears;

Our lives have been filled

With hopes and fears

Over the past

Twenty-plus years.

Even over the distance

Between us today,

I hope you feel

The smile I send your way.

Untitled #52

I do believe

It's safe to say

The good Lord

Shined a light my way.

It is by fate

And not by chance

We have started

This little dance.

Two lost spirits,

Walking the earth alone,

Searching for a partner

To call our own.

We talk like

We will never part;

I do believe

You've stolen my heart.

Untitled #53

I will take

Your breath away.

What will you do with it?

You might say.

I'd bottle it up

So that I could say

I captured the breath

Of an angel today.

I hold you in my heart

As I desire you in my arms;

I want to sweep you off your feet

With all my witty charms;

I want to take you away

To a place where angels play,

Live out my life with you

As the days just melt away,

Hold you close to me at night

After we take time to pray,

Wake up every morning

With you and say

I love you more and more,

Each and every day.

Just to smell your hair

And to kiss your lips

To me, my dear,

Would be a trip.

Untitled #54

It has been too long

Since I've seen your face

Since I've felt your touch

And your warm embrace.

I have thought of you often

Ever since that day

You touched my heart

Then went away.

Once again I hope and pray

Our paths will cross again today.

A magical moment,

Captured in time:

I'm at a loss for words

In the middle of this crazy rhyme.

To look into your eyes

On that wonderful day—

I cannot wait

To send a smile your way.

I struggle most quietly

Deep down inside of me

To hold back the emotions
Bottled up in me with pride.
I have searched my whole life
For a woman like you to make my wife—
One with great conviction,
Cuddly, caring, and true.
Now it is
With patience I wait
For God to show me
Our final fate.

Untitled #55

It has been

So many years

With thoughts of you

In my hopes and fears

I want to touch your face

Wipe away those lonely tears

You are the one

I hold close and dear

Even with distance

Keeping us apart

You hold a special place

Deep within my heart

I haven't held you close

Or kissed your lips

Haven't felt the touch

Of your fingertips

Something draws me closer

To you each day

I know in my mind

You're just a dream away

I hope someday

To have you near

Hold you close

And whisper in your ear

That you are special to me

My dear

Untitled #56

I want to

Make you smile today

So I am sending

My heart your way.

Please hold it close

And take care of it;

Someday you will see

I'm not full of it.

At times I stumble

And may even fall,

But it is you, my dear,

Who is the key to it all.

I dream of a life

Tried and true,

A life that can only

Be shared with you.

So hold onto my heart,

And keep it near,

Because you are the one

It belongs to, my dear.

You are the light

That warms my heart

Even though

We are worlds apart.

Your smile shoots through me

Just like a dart.

You had my attention

Right from the start.

Your smoldering eyes

Take me away,

As close to heaven

As I'll get today.

Please don't turn

Or run away;

Lost in your eyes

Is where I want to stay.

To hold you in my arms

And kiss your lips;

To touch your cheek

With my fingertips…

Please grant my request

So that I can say,

"Jesus, you may come now

And take me away."

Untitled #57

Deep down in my heart

There is a love

For a woman as sweet

As a snow-white dove.

Her smile alone

Makes me feel complete;

It warms my whole body

From my head to my feet.

The look in her eyes,

To which no one can compare,

Just blows me away

Like the wind in the air.

The touch of her hand,

The warmth of her hugs:

They make me melt—

She is my ultimate drug.

She doesn't even realize

How amazing she is;

That's what makes her so special

And the woman that she is.

My hope is someday

To hold her in my arms

And make her feel safe

From all the world's harms.

I vow today

To never let her go

And to show her a love

That will continue to grow.

Untitled #58

You truly are something beautiful,

A wonderful sight to see:

A snowflake falling from the sky,

A piece of heaven brought down to me.

Your caring and compassion

Have touched me from afar.

You are quite amazing,

Just like a shooting star.

You are my special snowflake:

Gentle, delicate, yet very strong

You hold your shape and composition,

No matter the wind that blows you along.

Someday I will see you again,

And we will be face to face;

I will be able to touch your cheek

And hold you in a warm embrace.

Think of it as a piece of me

Holding you close and dear

Because you truly are something beautiful,

A wonderful woman—that is clear.

You are my wonderful snowflake,

And I am closer to heaven when you're near.

Untitled #59

A gentle kiss,

A gentle touch:

These are the things

We love so much—

Heaven isn't so far away.

A gentle breeze,

The warm sunlight,

Someone to love

And hold all night—

Heaven isn't so far away.

That brunette hair,

Eyes dark and deep,

Those ruby red lips

And smile so sweet—

Heaven isn't so far away.

To hear her talk,

To touch her cheek,

To see her walk,

She is so complete—

Heaven isn't so far away.

I look so deeply

Into her eyes;

It really comes

As no surprise

That heaven isn't so far away.

Untitled #60

If you have ever been a dreamer,

Then I guess you know it's true

That when you dream of someone,

It's like they're there with you.

I often dream of love,

But it may never come true:

That I get to spend my days and nights

Standing right next to you.

If only I could see you smile

And look into your eyes today,

It would lighten the load on my heart

And take away these shades of gray.

I will always be a dreamer—

This I know to be true;

Even after I find you,

I will still only dream of you.

I promise not to forsake you

I will try not to make you cry

I just know I want to be with you

Until the day I die.

We will walk through life together

And give love another chance

I will hold your hand through every adventure

And we will share a wonderful romance.

Untitled #61

Two hearts of God

Joined as one.

The moon shines bright

Over the setting sun.

With a gentle kiss,

A new life has begun;

The sun shines bright

For the joyful ones.

You and I

Sing like the sun

Together with Christ

And together as one.

Meant for each other

Since our lives were begun,

Now it is time

For God's will to be done:

Two joyful spirits,

An undying love,

Blessed in unity

By a voice from above.

Untitled #62

I look at you, girl;

You look at me.

Sometimes love

Takes time to see.

I sit alone, girl,

Right here in the dark

With dreams of holding hands

And walks in the park.

If I had to guess,

I'd say you knew from the start

Because your eyes shot arrows

Straight through to my heart.

I will rescue you, girl;

Will you rescue me?

If I could only know

Just how you feel,

I would know for sure

If this love's for real.

But I am afraid, girl,

To let my feelings show

So I guess for now

We may never know.

I will just look at you, girl,

And you can look at me;

This kind of love

We may never see

What it could

Or could not be.

Untitled #63

As time has passed,

It came to be

A gentle kiss

Was meant for thee.

Please do not run

Please do not flee

For I come to you

On bended knee.

It is my heart

I give to thee—

Oh please, fair maiden,

Hear my plea.

Your beauty is like the sun;

It will always be.

Your smile lights a fire

Deep within me.

Your love for God

Is plain to see.

You light up a room;

You captivate me.

By your side

Is where I wish to be;

My heart and soul

Were meant for thee.

It is you, my dear,

Who completes me.

Untitled #64

As sand drips through the hourglass

And I count the days away

I can't even begin to count

How often I have thought of you today.

Just to touch your hand

Or to be lit up by your smile;

With those darkened angel eyes,

You turn me like a dial.

To you I've told my secrets

That I kept under lock and key;

The world sees what's on the surface,

But you see the inner me.

But yet you still say

You just can't figure me out

And you sit and wonder

What it is I'm all about.

Well, my heart yearns for your heart—

I just thought that you should know—

And the only thing I want to be about

Is loving you from head to toe.

Untitled #65

While you were sleeping,

I thought about you today:

I thought about the time we had

And the dreams of yesterday.

Now I don't know

What to think or what to say;

Times have changed me,

And the dreams have gone astray,

Yet I still look forward to our first kiss,

And holding your hand one day.

I've often thought about you

Ever since you went away;

Some things you hold in your heart so deeply

That words can never convey.

The feelings I still have for you

When you turn your eyes my way

May not seem like much to you,

So I am turning shades of gray.

But the love I still have for you

Is still as young as yesterday.

Untitled #66

On broken wings

I try to fly;

Can I reach

The blood-stained sky?

I stand in awe

As she passes by

I try to smile

I contain my sigh—

If she only knew

How hard I'd try.

On bended knee

She makes me fly;

I know of her,

But she is not mine.

She holds my heart

Within her eyes

I've seen her smile—

Now I can die.

With lips of red

And dark brown eyes

She fills me up

As she passes by.

Untitled #67

Won't you be my shining star

In this world of darkness I call home?

Won't you be my candlelight?

For every fear I've ever known

Weeping willows fill my heart,

And I know I am not alone.

Wandering ripples fill my mind

For every stone ever thrown.

Two kindred and wandering hearts,

Traveling the world, all alone.

Plant a seed and get a start—

A blossom I've never known.

My eyes are filled with hope

That you'll send a smile my way

My heart will never break:

Love never came or went away.

I may not seem like much

In this world in which we roam

But to hold you close tonight

Is the thought that brings me home.

Lord Jesus, fill my heart
With a hope I've never known;
My faith brings me light
Of a love all my own.

Untitled #68

As sands drip though the hourglass,

I watch the time go by.

I've never even met you,

Not even to say hi.

The first time I ever saw you

Could have been a vision or a dream—

I wasn't sure you were real!

Things aren't always what they seem.

Then I saw your picture,

And it turned my darkness into day;

Now I just want to meet you,

So to the good Lord I pray.

I don't know what to make of it;

Could it be friendship or something more?

But I do know one little thing:

Your eyes I do adore.

Untitled #69

I believe I met an angel

Both beautiful and sweet

For when I looked into her eyes,

It felt like heaven was at my feet.

She may not truly be an angel,

But her smile lights my sky;

After one mere hug and kiss,

I didn't want to say goodbye.

I look forward to getting to know her

A little bit more each day—

Let the good Lord be our guide

Is what I hope and what I pray

As we build this friendship

With possibilities of even more,

Since she already took a piece of my heart

When God opened up that door.

So I enter into this next adventure

With open heart and open hands

For God designed a woman

To be beside a man.

Untitled #70

I hear your heart,

I breathe your breath.

Without your love

I wish for death.

I don't know;

Could it be true

That I was meant

To wait for you?

To hear your voice,

To touch your cheek,

To make you smile—

My life is complete.

I've dreamed a dream

Like lovers do;

Don't you know

Every dream is of you?

Come talk with me

Come walk with me

Just one woman

Just one man

Just one love—

It's in God's hands.

Let's dream a dream

Like lovers do

You dream of me

And I'll dream of you.

I just want

To hold your hand

Walk barefoot

And make no plans.

I'll keep dreaming a dream

That lovers do

Until the day

I am with you.

Untitled #71

Oh how I long

To see your face

To feel your kiss

And warm embrace

Just the thought

Makes my heart race.

Without you, dear,

I'll never find that special place.

I want your smile

To light my every day

I won't let a single moment

Ever slip away.

Within your eyes,

I see heaven in a special way.

Oh, how I long

To be with you today.

You're the angel

Of my eye;

I won't ever

Say goodbye.

It is you

Who makes me high

And with you

I wish to fly.

I don't care about

Your past;

I know that we

Can make it last—

We'll take it slow,

Not go too fast.

When they made you,

They broke the cast

'Cause you are

The angel of my eye

And it is you

Who makes me high.

Untitled #72

We talked all night

Right from the start

Just like best friends

Sitting in the dark

I have yet to see

Your beautiful face

But still we talk

With amazing grace

A friendship started

With blinded eye

An always smile

A loving sigh

As we do

This little dance

My thoughts all swirl

On true romance

Yet to see

And yet to know—

Where oh where

Will this go?

Untitled #73

Pieces of my heart

I give to thee

Just like the flower

Gives to the bee:

A part of you

I wish to be,

Just like the bark

Is to a tree.

Our river of love

Won't run dry

My lips will never

Say goodbye

Together forever

We laugh, we sigh

As birds of a feather

Together we fly.

In this world

Of blacks and grays

Your smile is there

To light my day

Together as one

We will pray

From your side

I will never stray.

I don't know how

To make you see

That I was meant for you

And you for me

In God's hands

I will leave it be

With patients and anticipation

I will wait for thee.

Untitled #74

Ever since you've been away,

I've only dreamt of yesterday.

It doesn't matter what you say;

I will still love you today.

Ever since you came along

It's all been right and nothing wrong

In my heart where you belong.

Please, won't you sing along?

Ever since you went away

I only dream of yesterday.

Come on in, and won't you stay?

I want to be holding you today.

Sometimes I don't know what to do;

What I need is more of you

You're so honest and so true

I'm going to keep on loving you.

Ever since you've been away

I've only dreamt of yesterday

Simple words just cannot say

How much I love you today.

Untitled #75

To hear your voice

To kiss your lips

Touching hearts

And fingertips

Stop the flood

Hold back the pain

Within my heart

You will remain

Within the dark

I'll hold the light

I long for you

Both day and night

Untitled #76

Oh sweet Juliet,

I cannot forget

The way it was

When we first met.

We talked and talked

Like lovers do

Your darkened eyes

Cascades of blue.

Like a dew-drenched rose,

Tasting the morning sunrise,

I long for your presence

Before my eyes.

You're my north star,

My guiding light;

I search for you

Both day and night.

My heart bleeds

Without you today;

Yearning and waiting

For your return I do pray.

You're the blood in my veins

You're the air that I breathe

I'd give back the rest of my days

Just to spend one with thee.

Untitled #77

Oh how I want

To be with you, dear

You are the one

That I want near

Losing you

Is my fear

Because I want

To be with you, dear

I won't push

I wont shove

I'll just ask

The good Lord above.

With patience I will wait

Every day when I wake

No matter how long

It might take

Because you're the one

I want near

As I hold back

A tear—

No, I won't

Look away

It is with you

I will stay.

It's so hard

To concentrate

Without you

As my mate

Yes, I believe

It was fate

And you'll never

Be second-rate

Because you're the one

I want near—

Untitled #78

I don't know how

To make you see

That you, my dear,

Are very special to me.

I know it all seems

Very strange to you;

I cannot make you believe

That my words are true

Or that I am expressing

My true feelings for you.

I cannot blame you for thinking

I'm just full of it

'Cause I spent most of my life

Not being worth a shit.

I guess all I can say is

That I really do care

And even from a distance

I enjoy the time we share.

Untitled #79

A simple little present,

Wrapped in gold and blue

Just to let you know

That someone cares for you.

I hope this makes you smile

And puts a twinkle in your eye,

'Cause when I think of you,

I know I will never say goodbye.

I hope that I have touched you

The way you touch me everyday.

Now I know you're turning forty,

And I really don't know what to say

So I guess that I will end this

With a simple praise to you:

You're fit, you're fab, you're forty—

And God still has plans for you!

Untitled #80

I am not

Going anywhere;

With you, my dear,

No one can compare.

You may feel differently

Than I do

But I was built

To be with you.

As a friend or a lover,

I will be by your side;

I will not continue

To run and hide.

Through the pain and the suffering,

Through the good and the bad,

I want us to share together

The dreams that we've had.

Our lives are not easy;

We are challenged every day.

From me, my dear,

Please don't run away;

I only ask that you

Share with me.

My loving heart

Will help set you free.

We are both lost souls,

Always feeling alone;

Our only contact

Is by telephone

But yet I wrap you

In my arms everyday;

I know you feel the comfort,

Even a thousand miles away.

Maybe it was meant

To be this way—

For us to comfort one another

From far, far away.

Don't shut it off,

But hold it close

Because it is for you, dear,

I propose this toast:

"You touch my life,

And I hope I touch yours.

I hope we continue to do so,

Throughout the years.

Please don't push

Our fate away;

Even from a distance,

You make me smile today."

TNC

Tiffany Nicole

My heart and soul

My baby girl

My rock and roll

Oh, how I miss

And love you so!

My heart bleeds

Since you've been away

There are so many things

Words just can't say

You'll always be

Within my love

My little girl

My angel dove.

Sometimes I don't know

What to do

So I hope and pray

And think of you.

No matter what

You think or say

No matter how long

You stay away

I will continue to love you

In every way.

Untitled #81

You make me better

Than I used to be.

You are my flower;

I am your tree.

When it storms

Or when it rains

I'll provide you shelter

From the pains.

Leaves may fall

From my tree,

But for every last petal,

I will rescue thee.

I've watched you blossom,

I've watched you grow;

I love you enough

To let you go.

You are my flower,

I am your tree;

You make me better

Than I used to be.

I will rescue you,

Because you rescued me.

Untitled #82

My heart bleeds

In shades of gray

Ever since

You went away.

Darkness falls

Across my brow

I toss and turn

And wonder how.

My tears are

My smile now,

My lost and lonely

Solemn vow.

Will this fog

Lift today?

Will I see

The light of day?

Will your smile

Pass my way?

Will I talk

With heart or head

Or hold my silence

Until I am dead?

Has God accursed

My tender heart?

A love so close—

Yet miles apart.

You say stop,

And I say start.

If we'd let our wills go,

I know we'd never part.

Untitled #83

But yet I die

Again today

For my love,

Has gone away

It does not matter

Night or day

Those are wasted

Words you say

Now the darkness

Guides my way

Now I stumble

Through today

Because my love

Has lost its way

Will the darkness

Become my light?

I'm not sure

What's wrong or right

Just need to make it

Through tonight

Make Christ

My guiding light.

I sing praise

To you each day

Because you help me

On my way.

Beside me

As my friend

I know we'll make it

Through the end.

As you guide me

On my way

You bring light

Into each day.

I know you'll never

Go away

And I thank you, Lord,

For each day.

Untitled #84

Sometimes it's hard to hide

The way I feel deep down inside.

Wish you were by my side—

Gosh darn my foolish pride.

I miss how we laughed and played;

I still remember it like it was yesterday.

We would watch and we would cry

And we would just let time go by.

So comfortable with you

I didn't have a clue

Until there came that day

You said, "We need to step away."

Now I sit and wonder why—

It doesn't matter; I just sigh.

No matter what I do

It seems my heart belongs to you

So I kneel down and pray

God will bring you back someday.

Until then I will dream of you,

Because that's all that I can do.

I know it must be true

That my heart belongs to you.

Untitled #85

Your brown eyes

Mesmerize.

You rock my soul;

I fantasize.

In a world filled

With mostly lies

Your honest spirit

Makes me realize

That in a dark world

Filled with shades of gray

A rainbow finally

Came to stay.

Whenever you send

A smile my way

It's like sunshine

On a cloudy day.

Presence

That one special moment
That makes dreams come true;
That one special moment
Meant for me and you.
That special buried treasure,
Found within the heart—
Oh! Can you hear that?
Let the music start.
Your eyes bind me, speechless;
I can't find words to say.
The hours pass like minutes;
When you hold my hand, I pray:
"I know she came from heaven,
But I hope you'll let her stay."
Sleep was never a thought
As night turned into day.
Every breath I take
Comes with hope so true;
Whenever my heart beats,
It's filled with love for you.

After I Found Christ

Wow what a journey it has been. I have realized many things since I found Christ. The most moving of all was that he was with me even when I wasn't with him. How great is that? I wake up each day knowing, no matter what life brings my way, there are better things to come. God Bless you all and I hope this section brings joy to your heart.

I know also by know, if you have been reading this book, you are wondering. What does all this have to do with pickles? In retrospect pickles have always been a part of my life. As a young boy playing baseball, we played a game we called pickle. Two boys have gloves and a ball and the third boy is in the middle trying to get to a base before getting out. Throughout life I have always seemed to get myself into trouble or pickles at times. As an adult I enjoy gardening and can pickles as well. So I hope you understand the pun on pickles.

Untitled #86

It was not by chance

But through God's grace

That we came

To this place.

I have met with Satan

And shaken his hand—

Me, a simple,

Mortal man.

But now it is

For God I reach.

Jesus died

To make us complete.

I have faced many trials

Along the way

That have made me

The man I am today.

The Journey

Pain, loneliness,

Self-destruction, and despair—

If I were to die,

Would anyone care?

I turned my back

On God one day

Because of all the hurt

I felt he brought my way.

I wanted to grab a hold of something

That I could see,

But ended up bottling all my emotions

Deep down inside of me.

Feelings of distrust,

Deceit, and shame,

For all of which

I am to blame.

But God never

Turned me away;

Jesus held my hand

Along the way.

He knew before
I ever turned away
That I would be back
Again some day.
Now I walk with Jesus
Each and every day
And I feel God's presence
Within me that way.
The pain and loneliness
Were all for naught;
Self-destruction and despair
Aren't even a thought.
I will keep God
In my heart and soul every day.
I know that Jesus will lead me
To the gates of heaven one day.

Untitled #87

All glory

Be to God

Who does not carry

A staff or rod.

He gave to us

His grace

We are His

Mortal race.

His son Jesus

Died for our sins

So that we could be

With him again.

So accept Jesus

As your savior

Because God does not

Require any favors.

He accepts us

As we are

Even as a sinner

Bellied up to the bar

Or the shining light

Of a shooting star—

God will accept you

Right where you are,

No matter how near,

No matter how far.

Untitled #88

I do believe

It's safe to say

That someone

Has died today:

They have been lifted up

Been taken away

To a place

Where angels play.

Oh, how I hope

And how I pray

That will be

Me someday.

I often wander,

But I never stray

For I belong

To God each day.

I hope that you

Will also pray

That more lost souls

Find God today.

Untitled #89

Did I die again today?

Has my gentle heart been torn away?

I have no pain; all feeling's lost—

A mental and emotional holocaust!

No more drinking, no more drugs

My skin starts crawling like I'm covered in bugs

My eyes don't blink; stone is my face;

My life is filled with such disgrace:

I've lost family, friends, kids, and wife;

All I have left is a dead man's life.

I never thought I could turn my life around

Then I caught a glimpse of His thorny crown

I fell to my knees, my face hit the ground

I was completely alone—there was no one around

Right there by the pond, I started to pray:

"God, please don't let me suffer any more this way!

Release me from my pain and demons today.

I don't want to be alone come judgment day."

He said to me, "Just let me in.

Open your heart to me again.

I sent to you my only son;

He walked with you since before life began.

He died on the cross for your human sins

Because I want you to come live with me again."

Untitled #90

It is within

His grace and glory

That I live

To tell this story:

Where

Broken spirits lay

We will never know

The price they paid

And we may not know

The deals they made.

For their

Unholy graves.

We can't just wave

And say goodbye

For they lost that twinkle

In their eyes.

From the Spirit

They walked away

Because of the pains

Of yesterday.

It's okay

To shed a tear

For all

Our friends lost in fear;

Can we

Just stop and pray

For all those souls

Lost today?

Don't be afraid

To grab a hold

Of something

So strong and bold.

Let us all

Just stop and say

We love Jesus

Again today

Untitled #91

I feel your strength

Within me now

I feel your love

Your solemn vow

With your love

I will not fail

I tried life without you

To no avail

You give me your love

And I give you mine

Not just now and then

But all of the time

It is with your love

I have begun to shine

I am not afraid anymore

To walk the line

You give me direction

And guidance from above

You, my Lord,

Are my one true love

With you in my heart

And you in my mind

I dream everyday

That heaven I will find.

Untitled #92

When I close my eyes,

I see your face.

I open my heart

To your warm embrace,

Your touch, your feel,

Your amazing grace.

Sometimes I just want

To leave this place

To be in your presence

Face to face

Our relationship

Will never end;

I remember when you

Were my only friend,

The thought, the feeling

That all was lost

Until I knelt down,

And touched that cross.

You took all my sins

And washed the pain from my face

With your touch, your feel,

Your amazing grace.

I opened my eyes

To a new world today.

My life from before

Has finally passed away.

Crucified—

You, for me—

Rose again

Alive within me.

Faith in you

Has set me free

To live the life

That was meant to be.

The blood, the body,

That thorny crown:

I kneel in wonder

At the joy I have found.

I acknowledge your presence

Within me today

The length that you went

Wiping my sins away.

In my fleshly body,

We live now as one;

From this day forward,

A new life has begun.

I feel your love

Deep in my soul

I smile in completeness:

You paid it in full.

Untitled #93

When I think of you, Lord,

Sometimes I don't know

What to say

Or where to go.

You made

The little drops of rain

You made

The hills roll in your name

You made the flowers

And the trees

You made the oceans

And the seas

You made

The sky up above

You made

A thing called love:

Unconditional

As it may be

I never thought

It was meant for me;

I was a sinner

Through and through

Never realized

What your love could do

Until

That fateful day

I asked you

To take my pain away.

You came

And rescued me

Lifted me up

And set me free

Now all I want

And all I will be

Is more of you

And less of me.

Untitled #94

Jesus talked to me today,

And told me he loves you.

He has a personal relationship

Waiting especially for you.

He came to earth and died one day

For the sins you could not bear

And no matter where it is you are

He is always there.

He wants to get to know you—

This I know is true;

He wants to wrap his arms around you

And let you know his love is true.

Untitled #95

If you open your heart

You may find

A way to leave

This world behind.

Unlock your thoughts

And free your mind;

Close your eyes

Love is blind.

Jesus came;

For your soul he fought;

Please don't make it

All for naught.

Accept his touch,

His warm caress;

Within his blood,

We find our rest,

Our pain and suffering

Washed away.

In broken bones

And blood he lay;

With his last breath,

He began to pray—

Not for himself,

But for your soul that day.

Untitled #96

Perfectly imperfect

A swirling stream

Keep the balance

Keep the dream

Rivers to brooks

Pebbles to streams

The water is clear

Your rocks, he cleans

No beginning or end

Just ways and means

Lay me down

Cleansing stream

Rocks to pebbles

Pebbles to sand

Reaching out

Touch my hand

Babe to boy

Boy to man

Man to babe

By a father's hand

Regenerate Us Lord

Like the caterpillar

To the butterfly

We need regeneration—

You and I.

It starts with hope

Of something new

Within our minds—

Me and you.

A little bit of faith

Within our souls

That there is a God

Who makes us whole.

A tingle of love

Within our hearts;

With Jesus Christ,

The changes start.

Let the Holy Spirit

Guide our way

Into truth, peace,

And love each day.

Through prayer, the Bible, and fellowship,

Circumstances abound;

Regenerate us, Lord!

We were lost; now we are found.

Through good and evil,

Our hearts became stone;

It took a vision of life

To know we aren't alone.

You put air in our lungs

And blood in our chests

Within you, Lord,

Our spirits do rest.

Through regeneration and anticipation,

We guide more people in

With the light you gave us—

That light from within.

Regenerate our hearts, souls,

And minds each day;

Our cares and worries—

We give them away.

Thank you so much, God,

For just who you are:

You're every ounce of energy

You're every last star;

It does not matter

How near or how far:

You're here to lift us up, Lord,

And heal every scar.

Untitled #97

Faithful, forgiving,

Fortress of salvation

Master of heaven

God of all creation

Father of our spirits

The heavenly lights

Strengthener of day

Comforter of nights

Rock Savior,

Glory and grace

Lord of the Earth,

Wiper of tears from our face

Advocate of confidence

Comforter in sorrow

Hope, light,

Writer of tomorrow

Our dwelling place

Our helper and our shield

Our judge and lawgiver

To whom all is revealed

Our redeemer, our refuge,

The potter of our clay

Strength of our heart

May we breathe you every day

Alpha and Omega,

Faithful and true

Jesus Christ our Lord

We give ourselves to You

Prince of Peace

Holy Trinity

Word of Life

We owe it all to Thee.

Untitled #98

Every night

And every day

For God's healing hand

I pray.

To be brushed

Across your gentle skin

And take away

All the pain within;

To heal your body,

Mind, and soul;

To once again

Make you whole.

Take them away, Lord,

Give them to me;

From these burdens of life,

Please set them free.

Chain me up:

My heart be bound

With a heart of love.

I kneel to the ground

I praise your name,

Sweet Jesus, today.

All these pains—

Just wash them away.

I will praise your name

No matter the cost!

Battered and beaten—

For me—

You died on the cross.

Untitled #99

Destined to fail

To no avail

Jesus Christ

The Holy Grail

One way in

And always out

The path is narrow

No room for doubt

Mothers and daughters

Fathers and sons

Sin after sin

Out of darkness we run

We stand to fight

Only using the Word

Together with Jesus

Free like a bird

Untitled #100

Will you come and follow me?

Will you come and follow me?

From the rustling of the trees

To the power of the seas—

Won't you come and follow me?

Yes, I will come and follow you.

Yes, I will come and follow you.

More than words can ever say

I know you love me more each day—

Yes, I will come and follow you.

Where you lead me, I will go.

Where you lead me, I will go.

The sun, the moon, the stars

I know you'll take me where you are—

Where you lead me, I will go.

Untitled # 101

I die to you each day

From the sins you washed away

When you hung upon the cross—

What we gained shan't be lost.

Untitled #102

When life was filled

With yesterday

It came and went—

Then went away

Just like the thoughts

Within my head:

One minute alive,

The next they're dead.

They say that it

Will be okay

But I just want

To go away.

Sometimes I don't know

What to do;

Then I wish

For more of you:

To feel your touch,

To see your face;

Forever love,

Amazing grace.

I'd never worry

What to do

If life were filled

With more of you.

You shine your mercy

Down on me;

Undeserving still,

But you set me free.

The life I live,

I live for thee;

From sin and death

You rescued me.

To feel your touch,

To see your face;

Forever love,

Amazing grace.

Untitled #103

Through whispering winds

I wait to see

If you, my Lord,

Will come for me.

Before your cross

I kneel and bow,

Your Holy Spirit

Within me now.

It is for you

I wait today,

To lift me up—

Take me away.

Through whispering winds

I wait to see

That you, my Lord,

Will rescue me.

Evolution

Sand to pebbles

Stone to rock

The cold, dead stare

Of a man in a box

A hardened heart

A lust-filled plan

Building walls

The broken man

Pain of others

Within his hands

The lifeless soul

Of a hopeless man

Rocks to stones

Pebbles to sand

Open the heart

Of a broken man

Living waters

Washed away

The painful life

Of yesterday

Washed away

The man that lived here

Yesterday.

Unworthy

At the foot of the cross

I sit today,

Unworthy to look—

So I will just pray.

Forgive my sins,

My devilish plots;

Forgive the things

I long forgot.

Through your grace,

I live today:

Another chance

To laugh and play.

Mend and knit

This broken soul;

Patch my wounds,

Make me whole.

Another lost fish

In a fishbowl;

Persistent love

Another saved soul.

You knitted me together

You birthed me twice;

Before I breathed,

You paid the price:

The first by flesh,

The second by soul.

You bridged the gap;

You make me full.

Rain on me

Again today,

Wash my cares

And worries away.

I walk the path

I stumble and fall

You help me up—

You paid it all.

Perfectly imperfect,

In every way,

Yet you hold me

And ask me to stay.

Untitled #104

A heart of peace

And not of war—

Shards of glass

Upon the floor.

A window to

The naked soul,

Without you

I was not whole.

You unlocked the doors,

Unlocked my mind

Walls and barriers

Left behind.

Shadows lifted

By a heavenly light,

I turn to you

Both day and night.

A crow a-searching,

A raven's flight

Behind the shadows

The heavenly light.

With open arms

I kneel and pray

Within you, Lord

I live today.

Memories of Liberty Point 5/19/14

As I look across

The morning sky,

I wonder only

Who am I?

Mountain ranges

And skies so blue,

They only could

Be made by you!

You painted lines

And loved each stroke,

A humbling presence

For us simple folk.

But yet you touch me

And help me to see

That all of this

Was made for me.

This moment in time

A planned event

Before I knew

It was heaven-sent.

John and Dave

And little old me

Basking in

Your trinity.

The valley below,

The mountains in view:

What blue skies connect,

Heaven runs through.

With eyes for you,

I see today

What Satan wants

To take away.

With blinded eyes,

I would not see

What you had planned

Just for me.

My heart, my mind,

My eyes—they race

As I stand still

In your embrace.

With gentle winds

You caress my face;

Let your sunlit warmth

Massage this place.

Captivated—

Yes, me with you;

Within every vision,

Your love is so true.

Your heavenly kiss

Upon each day;

You touch us all

In a special way.

I pray for the lost

And the unfound,

That they feel your kiss

And turn around.

Reflections of Liberty Point 5/21/14

Even though it's a desert wasteland,

It has beauty that lies within.

If you only look at the surface,

All you'll ever see is sin.

When you rush through the darkness,

Satan gets a win.

Through patience and perseverance,

I will stake my claim,

And you will come to see

Why Christian is my name.

Even as I sit in darkness,

A greater light will come to be,

And even in the valley of death,

A flower will reign free.

I sit and praise you

Through the darkness till the dawn;

In stillness I wait for you

To reveal what is going on.

I worship and I praise you

In love, truth, and song.

I will praise you in the darkness;

I will praise you in the light

I will praise you in this sinful world—

You are my every delight.

In my stillness I wait for you,

Your timing I anticipate;

I put away my desires

Because you never will forsake.

Untitled #105

You place your kiss

Upon my soul.

It's your caress

That makes me whole.

A peace instilled

Within my heart;

When I close my eyes,

The music starts.

Once a broken, lost,

And sin-filled man,

I stand so proud

Within your hand.

Perfectly imperfect

I am today

Opti-pessimistic

In every way.

When I close my eyes

I see the light;

I'm blinded by

That heavenly sight.

The winds caress

My human brow.

A peace within,

Never questioning how.

Vivid colors

Within my mind

Prepared to leave

This world behind.

I kneel and bow

And give thanks today

That my Lord and Savior

Is here to stay.

Lifegroup Retreat 9/16/14

Standing in the water at the beach of Camp Mac

Contour waves

And complex lines

A link between

Your world and mine.

Ever-changing patterns

Drawing me in;

You know where I started

And where I have been.

Your light caresses me,

Your wind does too;

With every captivating moment,

My thoughts are of you.

The light reflecting off the waves

Makes things much more clear

Even in the darkness

I have nothing to fear.

Intricate rocks, little pebbles,

Every grain of sand that is here:

You placed each one,

Holding all of them dear.

You watched me spiral,

Live life without shame,

Knowing in the end

I'd have myself to blame.

With patience you waited;

You watched day and night

Knowing someday I'd see

Your heavenly light.

Broken and battered,

I made such a stir;

Restored by your glory,

My heart becomes pure.

One rock, one sinner,

One heavenly light:

It is you I will follow,

And together we fight.

To think I once thought

I lived life alone!

But you're by my side,

And together we roam,

Searching for sinners

Lost in their own pain

Just to tell them it's true—

You love each one the same.

The fire that burns

Within will stay

As I kneel on the ground:

To you, Lord, I pray.

Bits and Pieces

These are unfinished poems I started. Maybe I will finish them later, but in the meantime, here is an opportunity for you to be the poet, see what you can do with what I started.

Untitled #106

Open up and let his spirit in.

He knows just what and where you have been.

Within his grace and love, you will be healed

As a new life to you is revealed.

It is hard to say how blessed I am:

I know the Son of God and the Son of Man.

Untitled #107

You trip

You fall

You get up again

You keep on going

And don't look for an end.

When you want to give up

Or you want it to end

Just spread your arms out

Again and again.

Open the heart

Break down the walls

God waits to catch him

When he falls

No worries or cares

No hidden halls

Kneeling before God

He standeth tall

From rocks to stones

From pebbles to sand

From living waters

Springs a new man

Always knowing

Right from wrong

What the Bible sayeth

He follows along

Holy Spirit

Guide his way

With Jesus Christ

He walks today

Living waters

Untitled #108

Will I ever love again?

Will heaven become earth?

Jesus died and rose again.

Lord, I thank you for rebirth.

Will I ever love again?

Will heaven become earth?

This life takes me to the edge

But I will always put you first.

Untitled # 109

Open hearts and open minds

A way to leave this world behind.

Untitled #110

For every drop of rain that falls

To God my Lord my duty calls.

Untitled # 111

To lose a life and yet be found

I see the light of chains unbound.

Untitled # 112

As everyone else runs away,

I know that you are here to stay.

Untitled # 113

Spinning in darkness

Again today.

Bring me your light;

Take me away.

Why do women

Affect me this way?

If it's a desire for love,

Please fill it today.

Why am I not satisfied

With your never-ending love?

I desire human contact,

Not just a touch from above.

Untitled # 114

Oh great Potter,

Mold me today!

Make me yours

In every way.

Touch my spirit

Fill my soul

Make me yours

Make me whole.

Untitled # 115

Fear within a wounded heart

Paintbrush stains with shades of dark

Whether holding on or letting go,

Why does it hurt me so?

Will the stains ever fade?

Broken-hearted barricade.

Untitled #116

Sometimes I just want to say,

Can I breathe my last breath today?

Can you lift me up again?

I seem to be at my wits' end.

Untitled # 117

Broken shadows

Broken dreams

Broken thoughts

Broken means

Afraid to share

Afraid to walk

Afraid to hurt

Afraid to talk

Untitled #118

When hearts, spirits,

And souls collide,

God will be there

To be your guide.

You have the strength

To push demons aside.

Don't run from your life;

There is no need to hide.

Untitled # 119

Your smiles and your eyes

Light the way

Deep into my heart

Each and every day.

Untitled # 120

My life is filled

With such decay.

Can flesh and bone

Just melt away?

Untitled # 121

He has peace within his spirit,

He keeps the wounded heart at bay;

Yet the wolf and the snake

Fight again today.

Untitled # 122

I am the fire in the night;

I am the dawn that lights your day.

Untitled # 123

I woke up breathing again today.

I really don't have much to say.

The pain of life hasn't gone away.

I forgive you for the things you say.

Untitled # 124

Deep, deep down

Within your heart

You can find

Where the shadows start.

They may subside,

But they will never part

From deep, deep down,

Within your heart.

Untitled # 125

I rage and I rage

And I can't turn the page.

Doesn't matter if I am alone

Or up on a stage

They want to lock me up

But I cannot be caged.

So I rage and I rage,

And I just can't turn the page.

Untitled # 126

Knitted in his father's hand

From babe to boy, from child to man

Never knowing what's in his plan

He starts to crawl but now he stands.

Untitled # 127

If your smiles turn to teardrops

And your pleasure turns to pain

If you're beaten, battered, and broken

Stand back and watch it rain.

Untitled # 128

You may think you're a flower on the wall

And that no one sees you there at all

But I am here to tell you and to say

Jesus sees you everyday.

Untitled # 129

Twisted words

Illusions spent

I still need money

To pay the rent.

The day is gone;

It came and went.

Untitled # 130

It does not matter what you say;

My past still haunts me yet today.

Light the candles, watch them burn:

Satan waiting at every turn.

Are you strong enough today

To make what's evil go away?

I kneel before you and I pray:

Make your words my sword today.

Untitled # 131

A broken man

Within your hands:

Was this part

Of your original plan?

Putting the pieces

Back together again.

Father of Grace,

I may never understand.

Untitled # 132

I am a candle in the darkness;

Lord, come and light my way.

Put a fire in my soul

And melt away my shame.

As you hung upon the cross,

You washed away my blame;

Your body and your blood

Spilled out just for me.

Your sacrificial love

Has brought me to my knees;

My heart weeps desire

Spilled out just for thee.

Untitled # 133

Broken hearts

And shattered dreams;

Life ain't always

What it seems.

Across the darkness,

Moonlight beams;

Pooling water,

Eventually streams.

Untitled # 134

Over the past seven years,

I have shed so many tears

Some in anger

Some in fear

But most because

You just weren't here.